FARMERS

PRANJAL BORKAR

Contents

I

Agriculture in India

India is an agricultural country. About seventy percent of our population depends on agriculture. One-third of our National income comes from agriculture. Our economy is based on agriculture. The development of agriculture has much to do with the economic welfare of our country.

Our agriculture remained under developed for a long time. We did not produce enough food for our people. Our country had to buy food-grains from other countries, but the things are changing now. India is producing more food-grains than its needs. Some food-grains are being sent to other countries. Great improvements have been made in. agriculture through our five year plans. Green Revolution has been brought about in the agricultural field. Now our country is self-sufficient in food-grains. It is now in a position to export surplus food-grains and some other agricultural products to other countries.

Now India ranks first in the world in the production of tea and groundnuts. It ranks second in the world in the production of rice, sugarcane, jute and oil seeds. Till recent past before independence our agriculture depended on rains. As a result our agriculture produce was very small. In case the monsoons were good, we got a good harvest and in case the monsoons were not good, the crops failed and there was famine in some parts of the country. After the independence our Government made plans for the development of its agriculture.

Dams were constructed across many of the main rivers and canals were dug out to provide water for the irrigation of the land. Tube-wells and pump-sets were provided to the farmers to irrigate the fields, where canal water could not reach. The use of better seeds, fertilizers and new techniques in agriculture, has brought about a revolution called the Green Revolution in agriculture. Our agriculture produce has increased manifolds, but the progress is still hot sufficient. Our population is growing at a fast rate. Every year we have" millions of new mouths to be fed. We must check this fast growing population.

In the past irrigation facilities were not sufficient. Farmers depended mainly on rain water for irrigation. Canals and tube-wells were very few. Under the five year plans our Government has built dams on many of the rivers. Bhakra-Nangal Project, Damodar Valley Project, Hirakud Dam, Nagarjuna Sagar Dam, Krishna

Sagar Dam and Mettur Dam are some of these dams. Water is stored in big lakes and reservoirs for generating electricity for our industries and agriculture. Water of the dams is being taken by canals to distant lands for irrigation. Tube-wells and pumping sets have been supplied to the farmers. Now more land is irrigated and better crops are produced.

Our land was loosing its fertility being put to cultivation continuously for years together. Cattle dung which is the best form of manure, was being used as fuel. The use of manures and fertilizers helps to restore the fertility of the soil. Our Government has set up fertilizer plants at Nangal, Sindri, Trombay, Gorakhpur, Kamrup and Neyveli. Many new fertilizer factories are being built. Some chemical fertilizers are being imported from other countries. The Government is supplying sufficient fertilizers to the farmers. The use of these "chemical fertilizers has increased our agriculture produce manifolds.

Our farmers were using the primitive methods of agriculture. -For years they have been sowing the seeds produced by themselves. These seeds were not quality seeds and the yield was low. Now high yielding varities from Government farms are being supplied to the farmers. These improved and better seeds have considerably raised our farm produce.

The area of the land under cultivation has been decreasing year after year. More and more land is required for building houses, factories, roads and other buildings. Therefore the area of the land under cultivation is decreasing. To meet this shortage more and more barren, waste and kullar land should be reclaimed and brought under plough. Our Government is reclaiming more waste land and it is-being brought under cultivation, by using proper chemicals and irrigation facilities.

Insects and diseases cause great harm to the crops. The crops must be protected against pests and insects to get proper yield. The Government is supplying pesticides and insecticides to the farmers at subsidized rates. The use of pesticides and insecticides has increased the quantity and quality of agriculture produce.

The soil has been loosing its fertility by the sowing of the same crops year after year. The rotation of crops is a good method to get better yield from the land. By changing the crop pattern the land remains fertile and produces better crops. The farmers have been taken up crop rotation.

Our farmers have been using old methods and old implements for farming. Our farmers have been using wooden plough for centuries. It could not plough the land quite deep. Now iron ploughs are being used. These ploughs can till the land deeper and prepare the field for sowing in lesser time. Banks and cooperative societies have given loans to farmers at low rate of interest. The farmers have bought new implements, fertilizers, improved seeds and farm machinery with these loans. A large number of farmers now use tractors for ploughing, sowing and reaping the crops. They have bought new implements for farming. The farming has become more easy and convenient. This has given a forward push to the agriculture production in our country. Now the Government is trying to educate the farmers. Agriculture colleges and universities have been set up. They give all type of knowledge regarding agricultural science to the young farm students. These colleges and universities organize orientation courses for the farmers. These courses train the people in modern techniques and methods of farming. The Doordarshan and Aakashvani are also educating the farmers regarding the new techniques in farming. They have started special programmers like Krishl Darshan and Kheti Ki Baten exclusively for the farmers.

The Government is trying to help the farmers in many ways. It has set up agencies like the Food Corporation of ·India to purchase the farm produce directly from the farmers at Government rates so that the farmers may not be fleeced by the middlemen.

Thus we see that every effort is being made to develop our agriculture and boost the agriculture production. We should not rest here. We should continue our efforts to develop our agriculture still further.

Now the Government is trying to educate the farmers. Agriculture colleges and universities have been set up. They give all type of knowledge regarding agricultural science to the young farm students. These colleges and universities organize orientation courses for the farmers. These courses train the people in modern techniques and methods of farming. The Doordarshan and Aakashvani are also educating the farmers regarding the new techniques in farming. They have started special programmers like Krishl Darshan and Kheti Ki Baten exclusively for the farmers.

The Government is trying to help the farmers in many ways. It has set up agencies like the Food Corporation of ·India to purchase the farm produce directly from the farmers at Government rates so that the farmers may not be fleeced by the middlemen.

Thus we see that every effort is being made to develop our agriculture and boost the agriculture production. We should not rest here. We should continue our efforts to develop our agriculture still further.

on their feet.

Minimum Support Price: This is another important policy that the government of India is keen to introduce. Whether its rabi crop or Kharif crops, fruits or vegetables, a minimum price will be set below which farmers shouldn't be forced to sell their produce. Usually, the farmers are taken advantage by middlemen at mandis and wholesale market where the produce is bought for very less price and then sold it to end consumers at a very high price, leaving farmers at a loss.

Short Essay on Agriculture in India in English

Below, we have provided a 200-word limit Agriculture in India Essay than can be used by students and children for school assignments and project works

Agriculture is not just a sector for India or just a job that people do, it is simply a way of life for us Indians. Without this sector, the population boom in this country and the economic cycles will come to a literal standstill.

As someone who has seen this sector closely, I can write my own personal opinion on this particular Agriculture in India Essay. A typical day in a farmer's life at a village consists of getting up early around 5 AM, taking a good bath at the natural streams nearby, having sumptuous breakfast, pack some healthy lunch and leave to the fields. From seed sowing, soil tilling, fertilising and harvesting the land, each and everything is done with love and care by the farmer.

Agriculture, having contributed for more than 15% of India's GDP and provided employment and livelihood for more than half the country's working population, hasn't got its due credit. The supports system that agriculture has given for India's economic prowess can't be described in just one simple Agriculture in India Essay.

Simply put, the amount of support a farmer has given to his country is more than the amount of support the country has given to its farmer.

II

Introduction to Farmer

Farmers are those who grow crops for all the countrymen, so the government should take necessary steps to protect them and their crops.

Also, farmers should get good prices for their crops so that they remain enthusiastic about their work. If they won't get good prices for their crops, they will migrate from the villages and there will be a dire problem of food for us in the future.If the farmers of the village move to the cities, who will do agriculture in the villages and who will feed such a large population.Therefore, it's necessary that we should work keeping in mind the rights of the farmers and take care of them.The condition of Indian farmers was very bad earlier. Earlier the farmers had to cultivate under the landlords.

The landlords had a lot of land, but due to a lack of knowledge of agriculture, they used to give their land to the farmers and entered into contracts with them. The contract was about an agreement that farmers would grow all kinds of crops on rented land and in return, they would get some share of the crop.

At the same time, it was also decided that whatever profit the farmer would earn, a part of it would have to be given to the owners of the land, which was very wrong.But, today it's not so. Today, farmers either cultivate in their fields or on leased land. Half of the crop produced from the cultivation done on leased land is given to the owner of the land and half is taken by the farmer.

Today, most farmers are educated, so no one can exploit them.The most formidable problem of the Indian farmers is that they get very less prices for the crops they grow, while the same crops are sold in the markets at two to three times higher prices. It's the main reason why most farmers are financially weak.Farmers are called the real heroes in our country because they are the ones who grow different types of crops throughout the whole year.Our entire agricultural system depends on these farmers. They grow crops according to the season and earn profit by harvesting them on time. Sometimes the crop is very good which gives them good profit but sometimes due to the uncertainty of the weather the crop gets ruined.The Indian farmer is not very rich so he leads a very simple life. They spend their whole life in farming. They are food providers for

us, so we should respect them.

III

Backbone of india

Farming is an age-old profession in India and millions are highly dependent on it for their survival. India accounts for more than 60% of the population which relies upon the income earned from agricultural activities and has the 2nd largest agricultural output in the world. Since India's independence, the agriculture sector has contributed more than 51. 9 percent to India's GDP. The Rural economic transformation in our country has been a reality with the increased modernization and market expansion. But still today, farmers are always unsure of the yield they'll reap. Considering this, there have been various plans and policies framed by the govt. for the betterment of this sector. Looking up at any recent research or facts about farming in India, we can easily witness the contracting progress in people's lifestyle indulged into this profession. Studying the prevailing dependency and sentiment of people in farming, we can easily end up realizing that problems are not properly realized and solutions offered are missing the targets. Without the proper intervention of government and responsible authorities, things are not going to trickle up positively for the agrarian population.

In the medium term, agriculture is a big challenge. There are weak monsoon and unpredictable weather conditions which adversely affect the income of farmers. But, even with better monsoons and adequate weather conditions, we have seen the income of farmers gradually coming down. Regardless of what the effects of monsoons or agricultural output does, farmer's income seems to be under stress. There is an urgent need to understand this issue and find better ways to raise the income level of the farmers. The prevailing issue of deteriorating farmer's situation cannot be dealt only with the process of rural transformation. With the government aiming to double the farmer's income by 2022, they need a determined run by the authorities at the ground level.

The problems in the prevailing irrigation infrastructure include the poor condition of rural roads which hamper the timely transfer and supply of inputs and outputs from the Indian farms. The lack of modern mechanism and cold storage, regional floods, inefficient farming practices, poor seed quality, which causes over 40% of farmer's produce going to waste. These are the major reasons because of which a farmer receive just 15% – 20% of the money which is being paid by the Indian consumer for the produce.

Considering all these serious issues, the government has been making efforts to enhance the prevailing situation through Market research and Information network, grading and standardization, developing agricultural infrastructure and constructing rural godowns. The government has also announced a 1.5 times higher MSP (Minimum Support Price) for 24 crops to giver better and improved incomes to the Indian farmers. A majority of Indian population surviving through farming often faces a backlash when it comes to the on-ground implementation of the roadmap for their welfare. The elevation of this issue has been a major reason behind the recent shift of young population from farming to jobs in the urban areas. We have witnessed a rise in the concern of the Indian government on this issue who is aiming for the holistic growth of farmers in the country. A commitment to eventually satisfy the aspirations and demands of farmers is being deliberately targeted through adequate planning which includes the use of digital platforms for transferring incomes, increasing the minimum support price, improving the awareness and education among farmers and providing satisfactory market exposure to them around the nation.

Farmers in India do countless hours of work to ensure that not only we but millions around the world, don't go to sleep hungry every day. The people who grow food for us are also the most undervalued in our country which should be a matter of concern for all of us. The Indian farmers do not have direct access to the government's procurement because of the corruption which has led the middlemen's to form a systematic approach and chain to directly abuse the farmers.

We have witnessed an unprecedented rise in the number of farmer's suicide in our country which has reached to more than 6000 per year. The ongoing scenario is not justifying the aim of the government to harness the potentials of the agriculture sector. A committed approach with a focused vision needs to be adopted for the holistic growth of the agrarian population in India.

IV

Indian Farmer

Farmers are the backbone of our society. They are the ones who provide us all the food that we eat. As a result, the entire population of the country depends upon farmers. Be it the smallest or the largest country. Because of them only we are able to live on the planet. Thus Farmers are the most important people in the world. Though farmers have so much importance still they do not have proper living.

Importance of farmers

Farmers have great importance in our society. They are the ones who provide us food to eat. Since every person needs proper food for their living, so they are a necessity in society.

There are different types of farmers. And they all have equal significance. First are the farmers who grow a crop like wheat, barley, rice, etc. Since the maximum intake in the Indian houses is of wheat and rice. So, the cultivation of wheat and rice is much in farming. Moreover, farmers who grow these crops are of prime importance. Second, are the ones who cultivate fruits. These farmers have to prepare the soil for different types of fruits. Because these fruits grow according to the season. Therefore the farmers need to have a great knowledge of fruits and crops. There are many other farmers who grow different other types. Furthermore, they all have to work very hard to get maximum harvesting.

The condition of farmers in India is critical. We are hearing suicide news of farmers every week or month. Moreover, farmers are all living a difficult life from past years. The problem is they are not getting enough pay. Since the middlemen get most of the money, so a farmer gets nothing in hand. Moreover, farmers are not having money to send their kids to school. Sometimes the situation gets so worse that they are not even having proper food. Thus farmers go in famine. As a result, they attempt suicides.

Furthermore, the other reason for the worst condition of farmers is Global warming. Since Global Warming is hampering our planet in every way, it affects our farmers too. Because of global warming, there is a delay in season. As different crops have their own season to ripe, they are not getting nourishment. Crops need proper sunlight and rain to grow. So if the crops are not getting it they get destroyed. This is one of the main reasons why farms are getting destroyed. As a result, farmers commit suicide.

In order to save farmers, our Government is trying to provide them with various privileges. Recently the government has exempted them from all the loans. Moreover, the government pays an annual pension of Rs. 6000 to them. This helps them to at least have some earning apart from their profession. Furthermore, the government provides quotas (reservations) to their children. This ensures that their children get a proper education. All the children should get a proper education in today's world. So that they get a chance to live a better life.

Farmers are the soul of the nation. Agriculture is the only means of living for almost two-thirds of the employed class in India. Farmers produce crops, pulses and vegetables which are needed by everyone. They work extremely hard so we can have food on our table every day. So, whenever we have a meal or eat food, we should thank the farmer.

Farmers of India are the largest producer of pulses, rice, wheat, spices and spice products. They are also involved in other small businesses such as dairy, meat, poultry, fisheries, food grains etc. According to the Economic Survey 2020-2021, the share of agriculture in gross domestic product (GDP) has reached almost 20 per cent. India has also emerged as the second largest producer of fruits and vegetables in the world.

Issues and Challenges of Indian Farmers and their Current Situation

Farmers face various issues and challenges related to agriculture. Some of them are poorly maintained irrigation systems and a lack of good extension services. Farmers' access to markets is hampered by poor roads, rudimentary market infrastructure, and excessive regulation. India has inadequate infrastructure and services for farmers because of low investment. Most farmers hold small areas of land due to which they are restricted to use traditional methods of farming and limit productivity. Whereas farmers with large pieces of land implement modern agricultural techniques and boost productivity.

If small farmers want to increase their production, they have to use good quality seeds, proper irrigation systems, advanced tools and techniques of farming, pesticides, fertilizers etc. For all this, they need money, due to which they have no choice but to take debt or loan from banks. They have an immense pressure of producing crops so as to yield profit. In case their crop fails, all their effort goes in vain. In fact, then they are not able to produce enough to even fill the stomachs of their families.

Change is happening in rural India but it still has a long way to go. Farmers have benefited from improved farming techniques but the growth is not equitable. The effort should be to stop the migration of farmers to urban areas. To make agriculture successful and profitable, it is vital that proper thrust be given to the improvement of the condition of marginal and small farmers.

Farming is considered as a noble profession and people involved in this profession for earning their livelihood are called as a farmer. Farmers are regarded as food providers for the people of the nation. They are the people who work hard on their farms without caring for the extreme heat of the sun, rain, or cold conditions of the weather. They grow different varieties of crops, vegetables, etc, and sell them at a reasonable price. These food products and vegetables produced by the immense labor of the farmers are used to meet the food requirements of the people of the entire nation.

The Lifestyle of Farmers

The life of a farmer is full of hardships and efforts. Farmers work hard every single day for growing different types of crops, looking after their fields to protect the crops from any type of damage. They live a disciplined life like a soldier, wake up early in the morning work for the whole day, and then sleep at night with tension for their crops in mind. They stop their work only for resting and eating lunch. They cannot relax and wait for their fortune like us. They do hard work without caring about the extremities of the weather conditions.

Despite providing the varieties of food to the people of the nation, the farmers eat very simple food and live a life full of simplicity. They earn the livelihood by selling the agricultural produce of their farms. They receive a very nominal price of their products after selling them. This small income is only the real earning of their hard work and dedication of every year. In this way, the farmers spend their whole life growing crops and waiting patiently for their harvest, and repeating this cycle again and again.

The Real Condition of Farmers in India

India is a nation that is recognized in the whole world because of its agricultural abundance. The credit of this appreciation of the nation in the whole world goes to the farmers of our nation. Farmers are the ones who make our nation recognized as an agricultural dominant nation by their hard work but they themselves are the sufferers and poor.

It is very sad to state that the farmers of India are financially very weak. They hardly manage to get two times meal. We all have heard about numerous cases of the suicide of the farmers because of the problem of money. They have to take loans and money from the money lenders and banks for accomplishing any of the bigger tasks like the wedding of their children, buying seeds for farming, etc. Their whole life is spent clearing their loans and debts. Such condition of the farmers who deserves a respectable position in our society is really painful. The government must ensure that farmers are provided with every benefit they really deserve for.

Why are Farmers Important for us?

Farmers play a major role in the life of every citizen of the nation. We cannot deny their importance in our lives. The importance of farmers in our lives is enlisted below.

Food providers of the nation - Farmers grow different varieties of crops, raise poultry, fishes depending upon the need of the people in different regions of the nation. Further, they sell their produce in the market. In this way, they provide food to all the people in the nation. Food is the basic requirement of our body. We need to eat the food as it provides us the energy to do different types of work. Whenever we are hungry we manage to eat something but never recognize the great effort that had been done by our farmers to make that food available to us.

Contribute to the economy of the nation - The different varieties of cereals, vegetables, fruits, flowers, poultry products, etc. are grown and sold by the farmers. This greatly contributes to enhancing the economy of the nation. India is already recognized as an agricultural economy in the world. The agricultural productivity in the nation is mainly contributing to the economy of the nation. Moreover, the export of several agricultural products also helps in increasing the economy of the nation. Thus it can be said that the farmers play a major role in raising the economy of India.

An exemplar for the people - Farmers are hard-working, dedicated, disciplined, and simple living by nature. They value every second of time and thus complete their every work related to farming on time. If they are not punctual in their life, they will have to face a great loss or damage of their agricultural productivity. They keep on working hard and waiting patiently for the whole year till the crops are harvested. Agricultural productivity is the result of their hard work and dedication. These qualities of a farmer make them an exemplar for us.

Self-reliant - Farmers are the food producers for the people of the entire nation. They eat what they grow and therefore are representing the quality of self-reliance. They are self capable of feeding themselves without depending upon anyone else for this.

Is the Condition of Farmers Really Pathetic in India?

We all have learned about the importance of farmers in our life. The fact that the condition of farmers in India is poor is really a depressing one. India is an agricultural fed economy and is getting the contribution of 15% by the agricultural sector in total GDP. The poor condition of the farmers of this nation is a notable point. The main issue lies in the old farming techniques used by farmers in India.

The government must try to disseminate and make the farmers aware of modern farming practices that require less labor and effort with a higher yield. This might help the farmers of India in combating the financial crisis they are facing. The government must announce several programs and policies that must benefit the farmers of our nation. These solutions can only help in eradicating the present problems of our farmers.

No Farmers, No Food !

He wakes up before sunrise and works in his field in every situation. Heavy rainfall, fog, bright sunny days, water crisis, climate change can't stop him from working in the field.

His whole family supports and helps him. They do all farming activities like ploughing, sowing, irrigation, harvesting, winnowing together.He makes the bare land fertile and create greenery on our planet. In any calamety we survive just because of efforts taken by a farmer.A farmer is a heart of any nation.If this heart stops working, the whole nation will live no longer. He not only provides food but also most of our needs are fulfilled because of his efforts only. It may be furniture, papers, cloths, medicines, cosmetics, raw materials to various factories and a lot more.

A farmer is the driving force to economy. It contributes about 18 % to total GDP as well as provides employment to 60 % of rural population.What if there would be no farmers?Imagine a day when there would be no farmers. We will suffer a food shortage.Meat industry is indirectly dependent on agriculture. If there would be no farmers, meat industry would face a major crisis.Not only this, some of the employments which are dependent on agriculture will decline. Grocery shops would be closed.Our late Prime Minister Lal Bahadur Shastri gave slogan 'Jai Jawan Jai Kisan' to emphasize the contribution of farmer to nations progress.No army in the world can win the war without food and all soldiers are provided by this basic need due to hard work of a farmer only.Many agricultural products are exported to foreign countries which bring foreign currency.This shows that the progress of country partially depends upon farmer's devotion. So let's give a salute and respect to the farmer.

Agriculture is one of the important sectors not just in India but in the whole world. This is especially true in an agrarian country like India where farmers are considered to be equal to God. Rightly so, because without farmers there would be no food to feed our growing population in the country. Almost every one of us would starve to death if the farming community stops their work. Undoubtedly, the farmer in India is the real backbone of our country. Without him, the economy would literally come to a standstill. The skyscrapers, shopping malls, fancy cars and other luxuries that people in the urban regions enjoy today only because a farmer in rural India is getting his hands dirty and working day in and day out in the fields.

Former Prime Minister of India, Lal Bahadur Shastri rightly coined the term Jai jawan Jai Kisan to hail both farmer and a soldier. A farmer is as important to a country as a soldier. While one protects the nation against enemies and guards the citizens against bad elements, another makes sure that we never sleep hungry even for one day. The food we eat every day is because of the sweat and hard work that our farmers go through in the fields.

But just praising farmers and the farming community is not sufficient. India has one of the highest farmer suicide rates in the country. And this precedence is not taken seriously by the people of the country and is never reported in any media channels. There are various reasons why a farmer commits suicide. One might be due to lack of proper production of crops due to scanty rainfalls or unpredictable weather conditions. Governments should intervene to help farmers cope up with their losses.

Waiving off loans that are given to farmers by banks is one of the solutions to decrease farmer distress in the country. But it's a short-term solution. Helping farmer with awareness programs about using technology to follow healthy agricultural practices and other modern methods to increase the production of crops should be done. Proper canals, dams and irrigation infrastructure should be built so that farmers can overcome the loss of unpredictable weather conditions to a certain extent, is a long term solution that governments should implement.

Another way in which farmers are taken advantage of is pricing strategy followed by the middlemen in the market. Farmers sell their produce to middlemen at an extremely low price and then middlemen sell the same product at high prices to the end consumers. Hoarding and black market of vegetables and crops are another menaces that are affecting farmers as well the consumers. Government has taken many steps to address the problems that are mentioned above in this farmer essay.

Minimum support price popularly known as MSP is a price that is guaranteed by the government for selling off the farm produce between the farmers and the market. This ensures that no middlemen will take advantage of there farmer and a minimum price is given to the farmer for his produce irrespective of any unpredictable situations.

Food Corporation of India (FCI) is an autonomous body in the country that buy crops directly from the farmers and store it in there cold storage areas for use during Emergency situations like wars or the one that we are facing now, COVID 19 pandemic. I would like to conclude by saying that the farmer and the work he does for his country is no less than the divine work. Governments should formulate proper policies and laws to take care of their needs. If we take care of his needs,

V

Pillars of nation

Farmers are the pillars of our nation. They work hard to supply food items for everyone living in the nation throughout their lives. In India, nearly two-thirds of the population relies on agriculture for their livelihood. They produce food, fodder, and other raw materials and are the major source of income for a farmer. Even though they are our lifesavers, the value that they receive in return for their efforts is very minimal. Many people loathe the profession of agricultural production and farming. One of the main reasons for such devaluing is the low profit earned by a farmer. People who value money over everything haven't yet realised the true value of a farmer. They are senseless about the fact that the food they receive on their table is the gift of farmers.

According to the Economic Survey 2020-21, agriculture has contributed 20 percent of the Gross Domestic Product (GDP) share. The food items made of wheat and rice are the major intake of people residing in

India. As a result, a majority of farmers in India are engaged in the massive production of wheat, pulses, rice, and spices. Other than these productions, some of the other agricultural activities of Indian farmers include the production of cotton, sugarcane, tea, dairy, sheep and goat meat, fisheries, poultry etc.

As an Indian citizen, it's joyous to announce that our nation is the world's largest producer of milk with 22 percent of global production and the second-largest producer of fruits and vegetables in the world. The total production of milk has made a very important contribution to GDP. Farming in India is never an easy job. Farmers should have a vast knowledge about the type of soil, climate changes, atmospheric conditions, and so on to receive the finest possible harvest. The food security of India highly depends on the production of cereal crops, fruits, vegetables, and milk to meet the needs of a growing population with rising incomes. For meeting such demands, a competitive production with sustainable cultivation techniques needs to be implemented.

Farmers are undoubtedly our national treasures. They play a very significant role in our economy. The life of an entire nation is dependent on the farmer. Do you know when National Farmers Day or Kisan Diwas is celebrated in India? It is celebrated on 23rd December to promote awareness among the people about the importance of farmers in a developing country like India. From 2001 onwards, the Government of India decided to celebrate it by highlighting the role played by farmers in the economic development of the country. 23rd December was chosen as the Kisan Diwas to commemorate the birth anniversary of Chaudhary Charan Singh.

Chaudhary Charan Singh was the fifth Prime Minister of India and had played a crucial role in shaping the agricultural sector by drafting various bills for the betterment of Indian farmers. He upheld the slogan "Jai Jawan Jai Kisan" of Lal Bahadur Shashtri and ardently tried to promote agricultural production in India.

Farming is never an easy job. It is a divine profession that requires extensive labour and effort. Even though farmers are widely proclaimed as the nation's most valuable assets, their real-life condition is far from ideal. Farmers face a lot of issues and challenges in India. Unexpected natural calamities like rain, drought, global warming, acid rain, and soil erosion are some of the regular natural mischiefs for farmers. For a few decades, reports of farmers' deaths have become very common. Breaking news of farmers' suicides is breaking our hearts. Despite the bills and amendments made by supporting the agricultural sector, the infrastructure is still inadequate.

Most of the farmers in India are small scale cultivators. Economically they are poor and hold very small areas of land for cultivation. Small scale farmers face multiple challenges and are restricted to using traditional farming methods. So, productivity will always be limited for them. As a result, the farmers will be subjected to immense pressure for getting profit from the production. If they want to increase their total production, they have to use good quality seeds, advanced technologies, pesticides and fertilisers, proper irrigation systems, and so on. To make all these practically possible, they meet their money requirement by taking loans from banks and borrowing money.

By following such procedures, farmers are actually taking a huge risk in their life as they couldn't predict anything about the harvest. Bad situations where farmers fail to produce enough profit to pay back their loan often leads to many of them committing suicide. The Government of India has taken several initiatives to stop such tragedies. Various schemes and policies have been implemented by the government so far for the betterment of farmers. But still, the issues in the agricultural sector are left tangled. As responsible Indians, it's our duty to save the life of farmers. Like the words of George Washington, "Agriculture is the most healthful, most useful and most noble employment of man." Let's start valuing farmers with respect and admiration.

Condition of farmers is critical in some parts of the world because some farmers have their piece of land, while some work on other's land and in that case there are middlemen who do not pay them adequate wages and take a good amount of money from them. Sometimes there is crop failure and farmers can't bear the loss, all this leads to suicide by the farmers. The government has taken many initiatives for them. The government came up with various privileges by providing loans and reservations to the needy farmers of our country to save the lives of farmers.

Farmer's life has been affected in many other ways such as coming up with globalization. The wave of globalization has made rich farmers richer and poor farmers poorer. Because of globalization and technological advancement, only rich farmers could afford high-quality seeds and advance technology which would reduce their labor, while the poor farmer could not enjoy these benefits. The geographical area of India is very huge and diverse, every land and location have their history and story. After gods, this country worships its crops and farmers. Farmers, all around the year dedicate their effort for the proper preparation of land and cultivation of crops for the whole country to eat. Farming yield is very significant in India and thus cannot be ignored; its proper role in this country's economy is quite the number. Farming also is a basic livelihood for a lot of people in this country and so the farmers are a really important society segment whose needs dictate the direction of the country. India is so agriculturally rich that it also exports the agricultural goods to a number of nations. Even with such huge agricultural wide and important area, Indian farming industry is a loophole for many farmers. Due to existing policies and unchanging old economic habits, farmers suffer the most. Famers suffer loss of crops, loss of money due to low prices (Prices which are undefined and unregulated), etc. The support of our government is of vital importance to the farmers of India. Many farmers yield good profit from their hard work but there remains a huge segment of farmers who are poor, poorer than when started only because of weak socio-economic policies and increasing corruption. Many took loans to support the cultivation of crops and due to some natural calamity lossed all their livelihoods and are forced to repay. Farming sector is both existent on organized level and unorganized one. The unorganized one is the dangerous one, it harms the farmers livelihood, threatens their future. The illegal land accusation by the mafia is a growing concern with which the government must deal accurately and with fierce force. The safeguard of our farmers is a priority we cannot ignore, and must protect their interests. Not just for the farmers, the agricultural sector can be a very big employment sector, a booming sector which can accommodate millions of people and jobs. It can be a very big boost to our country's economy. But even after all this, the farming sector of this country needs an efficient system for crop production, away from the traditional time consuming methods we can shift to more advanced forms of farming, this also requires government's support and supervision. But viewing from different perspective farming in India is dying, not in the food production wise but the desirability of farming as a profession. The reason for this is often the risky side to farming, one bad yield and no money, plus traditional farming is a very hard and laborious task making it more undesirable for the advanced generations.India is a country of villages. Agriculture is a major profession in this country. Therefore, a farmer places very important position in our social order. She is the backbone of our country. Hard work, patience and honesty are some characteristics of his character. He is so suffering that the people of his country are very rich. He is a very useful member of our society. She works hard, sheds her sweat and blood for the sake of her countrymen. He grows grains, vegetables and fruits for us to eat. She grows cotton from which clothes are made. His work is very heavy. He works from morning to evening. The life of his hard work and open air makes him hard and strong. He lives a simple life. He knows a lot about the quality of land, seeds, manure and sowing, water harvesting and crops. They have now started using modern methods of agriculture. Their food and dress is quite simple. She wears light clothes. She is plain, straightforward, loving and innocent. Its reasonably good income. She spends a lot on marriage and other celebrations and is often in debt. Our government is trying to improve them very much. He is no longer illiterate and superstitious. He is a respected person. He deserves a place of respect for society in a big way. An Indian farmer, in fact, is the backbone of the Indian nation.

ndian farmers so that they can improve their productivity as well as their lifestyle. It is my pleasure and respect to host this meeting. But before we continue our meeting, I would like to say a few words about Indian agriculture and our Indian farmers.

We all know this already that our Indian farmers are one of the most industrious farmers in the world. They spend the whole night to grow crops for the country and to provide different types of food to their citizens. Although they usually earn very little money but still they work hard with their blood, sweat and tears. Earlier there were no facilities or proper equipment for farming in agriculture, but now the proper facilities, as well as new techniques have been introduced. As the process of agriculture improves, the conditions of farmers will improve automatically. But today the condition of the farmers is very bad and they live by their burden of debt and many of them committed suicide due to this.

In India, about 11.2% of all suicides in the country are committed in the suicides of farmers. There were approximately 12,602 cases of farmers' suicides in the year of 2015 and 12,000 suicides have been reported every year since 2013. Therefore, the country still needs to protect these gems, which farmers prevent from taking their lives. The government has set up various policies and strategies to improve the situation of farmers in the country. In order to reduce the poverty among the farmers and increase their production, the government has improved the supply of electricity and water at concessional cost, which once blackouts the country in many parts of the country.

However, this was not the only reason for blackout, but the government came face-to-face with the decision to provide diesel to the pumping machine. Several programs have been started to educate the farmers about agriculture and new techniques, so that they can improve their productivity and earn profit. In the year of 2015, p. M. Narendra Modi announces doubling the income of farmers by 2022. In May 2016, the Indian government has set up a Farmer Commission to fully evaluate the agricultural program. The government is still on a mission to solve the problems of farmers and remove poverty from their life.

We always try to make everything the best and keep people's faith in our restaurant. As this day is very special, we have invited some people without whom we can not open a restaurant and yes! They are our great farmers. Today, we have organized a few things to make this event even more special for our farmers. But before starting with the event, I would like to express my feelings and beliefs about my hardworking farmers.

Opening the restaurant is not possible without the farmers who provide us raw food. They are the backbone of our country and are equally respected as soldiers in the country. There was a time when our country was known for its prosperous agriculture all over the world. Western countries were influenced by the diversity of crops and especially the variety of spices. In fact, we are living in a country where we have a uniform experience of every season of nature with different climatic conditions all over the country, which are different in the country and therefore our Farmers are able to grow different types of crops, weather and climate. We can find that every part of the country has its own distinctness, which differs from north to south and from east to west. We should respect this special gift of maternal nature which he has given us.

As we all are aware of the current situation of farmers in our country, we really need to support them and we should understand the importance of food in our lives and farmers should be appreciative of the efforts it has made in production because Every time we waste food, we disrespect the efforts of farmers. Although the government is taking some action to improve the situation of the farmers and to reduce the pressure on their back every day about those loans, children's education, family management etc., many people have to educate the farmers Programs have been started. Regarding the new techniques of agriculture and bank loans and policies, which have actually improved the conditions of the farmers somewhere and I hope this day will be better with the passage of time.

Indian farmers are the biggest reason for the pride of our country. They are the souls of our country. This incident is nothing but a way to show them and give them love and respect for which they deserve.

When we hear the word "farmer", the first thing that usually comes into our mind is hard work and dedication. He is perhaps the most industrious in the form of a soldier who is always ready to fight for the protection of the country. A farmer is a person who earns his income and his family very little earnings even after hard work and this is the truth of his world. Most of the time, they are not able to arrange food for their family because the amount received from their blood, sweat and tears is not enough. They have to pay lenders or banks to return many loans, provide education to their children, feed their families and meet many common needs.

There were many such cases where farmers took their own lives or committed suicide as it became difficult for them to arrange full meals for their families. They live the hardest life that we could not imagine. His concern for paying a loan for his family and providing me food twice a day gives him no choice other than suicide because the government's attention to their problems is not enough. It really feels bad that even after hard work, a person is not getting enough money to arrange food for his own family.

After looking at the factual situation of farmers, our country's government has introduced some policies and technologies for the agricultural sector. Appropriate facilities are being provided to farmers such as water, electricity, raw material or special bank loans etc at lower prices. Their children are being provided free education and food in government schools. Home loan is being provided to farmers with special policies so that they have a better place to live. Although there are still many places in India where farmers are not able to take advantage of these policies due to lack of proper implementation of the entire country, but if implemented effectively across the country, then these policies can change the lives of Indian farmers. Are.

VI
farmers

Life without food,
    Is like a tree without root.
    Life without food,
    Is like a bad dream come true
    Food comes from farm,
    These farms make our country charm,
    Our country's pride is hidden in farms,
But the growing population rings an alarm Farmers try their best to cultivate more, For lost ships to become a sea shore, These efforts will not be in vain, One day the dry land will also have rain THANKS to farmers for growing food! THANKS to farmers for giving our life tree roots!

VII
World without farmers

It's impossible to imagine a world without farmers. In this era of COVID-19, the economy of India was maintained by farmers of India. In a lockdown, we are all sitting at our homes safely, some farmers are working in the fields for us. Farmers play an essential role in developing the economy of any state. The government of India focuses on the activities of industrialization. Don't focus on farming activities. What will happen if everyone goes towards the world of technologies and diverts attention away from agriculture?

It is needless to say that farmers are an essential part of our society. There is no difficulty in saying this, and farmers work for us in the day-night to provide food to us. In some fields, big landlords take advantage of farmers, and these landlords reap the benefits of our farmer's hard work and their blood and sweat. In many countries farming is done on the tenancy.

The primary source of food is farmers, they are the main person behind the food chain. If farmers stop farming and other agriculture activities, we all face the major problem of food deficiency. All the supply of fruits and vegetables start from the hands of farmers and goes to each side of the county.

In the world, farmers are the only people that are always happy to feed others. In food deficiency, the economy of a country goes down, and all the development stopped at a single stage.

Farmers use the tractor and other agriculture equipment in their farming activities from which country wouldn't face food deficiency.

1. Food Deficiency

The primary source of food is farmers, they are the main person behind the food chain. If farmers stop farming and other agriculture activities, we all face the major problem of food deficiency. All the supply of fruits and vegetables start from the hands of farmers and goes to each side of the county.

In the world, farmers are the only people that are always happy to feed others. In food deficiency, the economy of a country goes down, and all the development stopped at a single stage.

Farmers use the tractor and other agriculture equipment in their farming activities from which country wouldn't face food deficiency.

2. Health Ratio Decreases

If there are no farmers, the health ratio of people will decrease, and the chances of getting sick will increase. It affects the economy of every country. In this modern world, food is available by the grace of farmers.

Farmers are always an essential part of our society and economy. All the structures of the economy based on the activities of farmers. To perform any business in the working world, it is essential to stay fit and healthy, and if we are not in a healthy condition, nothing is possible to do.

3. World's Economy Falls

If we imagine a world without farmers, then we reach a situation where if we try later, never stand back as the same as the before economic condition. Indirectly or directly, the whole world is dependent on all primary and advanced activities of agriculture. All the developed or developing countries lie in the same line at the economic status view due to the scarcity of farmers in the world.

Economic development is connected to the country's agricultural sector. It is one of the most significant processes to speed up development and enhance the country's standing in the world.

4. Rate of Unemployment Rises

The industry of agriculture is yet one of the largest sources of employment in all the world. In farming, there are plenty of jobs available, like working as a farmer, technician of farming equipment, ordinary workers, scientists, and many others.

In all developing and developed countries, agriculture jobs decrease the rate of unemployment and provide a large number of jobs in most sectors. It comes to decreasing poverty, evidence shows that focusing on agriculture is more adequate investing in other industries.

5. Effect on International Trade

The outcomes of agriculture cover a vast portion that traded Internationally. Most countries supply them, export them, and trade for materials they do not have. If any country suffers from the scarcity of farmers, prices increase, destroying the flow of trade.

India exports a good amount of agriculture products, and without farmers, agriculture products can't be supplied that will impact international trade. This will directly impact the economy of the country that will be affected badly.

We have seen a viral photo in the social media that a farmer sets fire on his paddy field due to the scarcity of day labours and low price of paddy comparing to production cost. Someone would like to say that any farmer did not set a fire on his paddy field in our country and this photo was taken in an area of Indian province. It might be true. Whatever the actual fact, scenario of farmers is not different than that in Bangladesh. The price of any product irrespective of categories should be higher than the actual production cost except exception.

This presumption is not rational for the products which are produced by the marginal farmers in our country. In Bangladesh, the marginal farmers mainly produce rice, jute, wheat, maize, etc in their own land or traditional rented land (Borga land). They devote their own physical and mental labours in their crops field expecting that they will fill up their own family needs of those crops up to the next season and remaining quantities will be sold to the market to gain. After ripening their crops, they discover that the value of their crops is lower than their production cost.

It seems that if he would sell his labour to others instead of cultivates the crops in his own or traditional rented land (Borga land), he would have gained. Yes, it is true that he could gain. By cultivating the crops, the gain is far-off; moreover, a farmer cannot take up his own labour cost which he devotes physically and mentally in his crops field. If it is continued, nobody prefers to cultivate the crops in our country. It will be seriously detrimental to our economy. Did we think what will happen in our economy if all of our marginal farmers stop the harvesting crops?

If all of our farmers stop the harvesting of crops gradually and move to other unproductive sectors, we have to import more quantities and we have to pay the price to the exporter in accordance with the international market price. It may be higher than the market price in our local market due to transportation cost. If we are able to import any products from abroad at the same price in Bangladesh, we can buy imported products at the same price as the local market. That is why we can wrongly think that we have no loss to import from abroad and there is no problem if marginal farmers will stop their cultivation the crops.

Seemingly, we have no loss; actually, we have to lose our GDP growth seriously due to the impact of outward remittance against import on the GDP. We should be aware that after adjusting Net Foreign Factors Income (NFFI) with GNP, we get GDP. So, GDP will reduce by the outward remittance and GDP is one of the major indicators used to measure the performance of a country's economy. We know that when a country performs better economically, citizens of that country will be able to enjoy a better life in many ways. So, considering GDP growth, we should not ignore the marginal farmers by any means.

In the rest of the world, the agriculture industry consists of harvesting all kind of crops, tree plantations, livestock feeding, grazing, raising fish and animal, dairy farming, logging wood, etc. Though harvesting crops is the soul of the agriculture industry, it could not able to gain the industry status in Bangladesh yet except cultivation of the tea plants.

The general perception is that harvesting is a work of poor, how it will be an industry? It is true in the perspective of Bangladesh in the sense that there is not enough land here to harvest commercially using modern technology by the industrialists. As a result, it is still familiar as a work of poor but it has a serious impact on our economy which we don't think necessary to feel.

Except for harvesting crops, all kinds of industries sell their products in the market at higher price of production cost to make profit since this is a thumb rule of any business in Bangladesh. It seems that industrialists always work for only profit, so they should not sell their products at below price of their production cost. Also, our Government supports them to gain profit by providing various facilities. Some of the cases, industrialists take various facilities from the Government by providing pressure in many ways like strike, press conference, meet with the Government authorities, turmoil, etc.

When the marginal people face any problem, we don't observe any effective initiatives taken by the government, because they do not have any association and lobbying to meet authorities. And they are not financially solvent enough to stop selling their crops as well as they have no any bank supports. Their main problem, they are poor and they have no power to obtain facilities from the Government. It has become a culture in Bangladesh. If a marginal farmer sells their crops at the price below production cost, why industrialist can't do it? They never do it because they are rich and they have power as well as many banks are ready to help them financially. This cannot be an acceptable policy in any country.

In the rest of the world except some other countries in Asia, they have huge unused land to harvest. They have no available labours but they have modern technology to support. They produce huge due to available land and some of the products, they can export to others country at the minimum price as their production cost is minimum for using modern technology and genetically modified organism. In those countries, harvesting crops is recognized as industry because industrialists/ rich men take lease/ rent the huge amount of land to produce the crops commercially.

In our country as well as overpopulated other countries in Asia, harvesting did not introduce as industry except tea plants because there is not enough land to take lease by the industrialists. Though, agriculture is the main profession of our citizens and harvesting crops is one of the major factors in our economy, the Government should take initiative to keep existence this profession. If we think individual production of farmers, it may be a small scale but cumulative production of our marginal farmers are huge and it has a great impact on GDP.

Also, marginal farmers should be provided the privileges to sell their products at higher price than the production cost, like other industrial products. Unfortunately, they cannot do it due to lack of finance and other setbacks. Considering their rights, contribution to the national economy, the government should take initiative to keep the price higher than the production cost. It may be done by fixing the price, or the farmers may be provided concession.

VIII

Agricultural practices

Agriculture farming in India is a century-old activity, and is currently the highest contributor to the GDP of India. Agriculture remains the largest contributor to the country's GDP and farmers constitute 58% of India's population. It means much of India remains untouched by the mindlessness of consumerism. Under its Agriculture Export Policy, the Government of India aims to increase agricultural export by over $60 billion by 2022. This means, the agricultural activity in India will be doubling. If we describe the farmers of India, they constitute 58% of the country's population. Agriculture is the primary source of income for the mentioned percentage of the population.The Indian food industry also aims to grow by leaps and bounds. Already, the Indian food market stands as the 6th-largest globally with food processing covering over 32% of the country's food industry. Thus, we see that India is enriched by both traditional and commercial forms of agriculture.

Agricultural Methods of the Indian Farmer

Agriculture farming in India is the oldest activity and has been the major livelihood for farmers. Over the years, farming methods in India have changed, thanks to the technology invention making the lives of farmers easy. Socio-cultural practices, climatic conditions, and other aspects have also contributed to the innovation in Indian farming. Currently, both traditional farming methods in India and modern farming are practiced.

Primitive Farming - One of the oldest techniques in India, primitive farming is practiced in small farms with traditional instruments like a hoe, digging sticks, etc. Farmers depend upon soil fertility, environmental conditions and other factors like heat for the harvest. This method is usually employed by those who use the output for their consumption. This technique is also called "Slash and Burn" farming where farmers burn the land once the crops have been harvested.

Subsistence Farming - Cultivation takes places across wide and larger land areas with two types of crops : wet and dry. Wet crops include paddy and dry crops grown are wheat, maize and pulses. This method demands extensive use of chemical fertilizers and different methods of irrigation.

Commercial Farming - This technique is a modern day farming method where the farmers use a variety of new-age tools for surplus profits. Insecticides and fertilizers are also used because the crops grown are spread across large patches of land. It contributes a great percentage to the country's GDP. While farmers in Haryana, Punjab and West Bengal practice commercial farming techniques, farmers of Orissa continue to prefer subsistence farming for large productions.

Plantation Farming - It is another subset of commercial farming. It makes use of both labor and technology to ensure the process is sustainable as plantations are spread across huge patches of land. It includes both agriculture and industry because of the nature of the crops grown.

Agricultural Practices: Food is a major requirement for all species to exist. But have you ever wondered how the food is grown? These all happen because of agricultural practices. The small plots of land are used for growing food that not only provides nourishment to animals but to humans as well. Good agricultural practices have been adopted since ancient times.

Implementing good agricultural practices is extremely necessary for a country like India to improve the food supply chain. Furthermore, it is the agricultural practices that play an important role in making farming easy and efficient. In the article below, we have provided information regarding food practices

Steps of Agriculture Practices

Let us go through each step in detail:

1. Landscape Management: A landscape is the apparent factor of a land, its landforms, and combined features of natural or artificial elements. Landscape management includes maintenance and implementation of physical elements, water bodies, land cover, indigenous vegetation, human elements, structures and buildings, and climatic conditions. Landscape management is of great significance in agriculture. Therefore, it is the first in the list of agricultural practices.

Soil is a critical natural resource. Soil is the earth's thin surface layer composed of mineral particles formed by the breakdown (weathering) of rocks, decayed organic materials, living organisms, water, and air.

Soil formation occurs through a variety of processes, including weathering of rocks and the mixing of rock materials with organic debris produced by plant decay; another process is a slow chemical alteration of water that seeps through weathered rock material after rains. Let us investigate what is causing the weathering! Weathering is the breakdown of rocks into smaller particles that eventually form soil.

Preparation of Soil

- In traditional agricultural practice, the soil is the primary substance for the formation of tasty and healthy vegetables. It is a necessary procedure before planting crops and sowing seeds to improve the soil.

- To increase the nutrients in the soil, various methods are used. The soil contains both living and nonliving organisms that are necessary for crop growth and development.

- Earthworms, microorganisms such as nitrogen-fixing bacteria, decayed organic matter, and other organisms are among the existing components. The minerals, nutrients, and water that the roots absorb from the soil are examples of nonliving components.

- Before the crop is planted, three major steps are taken to prepare the soil: ploughing, levelling, and manuring.

- Loosening and turning the soil is done through ploughing (tilling). Before sowing the seeds, it is necessary to loosen and turn the soil in the fields in order to break it down to the size of the grains, which is accomplished with the help of three main ploughing implements or tools: hoe, cultivator, and plough.

Ploughing also brings nutrient-rich soil to the surface. Ploughing can also be used to integrate manure, uproot weeds, remove infectious pathogens and insects, and so on. Ploughs made of wood or iron are used for this.

tractors or bullocks pull this plough. A hoe is another tool for removing weeds and loose soil. After ploughing, the soil is evenly distributed and levelled in the field.

Ploughing advantages

Ploughing loosens the soil, allowing nutrients from deep soil to rise to the surface.

Ploughs made of wood or iron are used for this. tractors or bullocks pull this plough.

By enabling more air to enter the soil and facilitating easier root penetration, soil aeration will increase.

Another tool for removing weeds and loosening the soil is the hoe.

Ploughing can also be used to integrate manure, uproot weeds, remove infectious pathogens and insects, and so on.

Soil Leveling

Following ploughing, the soil must be levelled. Crumbs are large lumps of soil that may be found in a ploughed field. The soil lumps must be broken up with a plank or an iron leveller. The field has been levelled in preparation for seeding and irrigation

Modern Farming Methods in India

Besides the above-mentioned farming techniques in India, there are other methods followed in different regions of the country. Much of these don't fall under traditional farming methods in India. This includes:

Aeroponics System

Aeroponics is the process where plants are grown in the air or mist environment without the use of soil. It is the subset of hydroponics, and suspends the plant root in the air to work. Farmers, by using this method will have better control over the amount of water to use.

Aquaponics

Aquaponics is a closed-loop system that relies majorly on the symbiotic relationship between aquaculture and agriculture for fertilization. This farming method combines conventional aquaculture with hydroponics.

Hydroponics

The hydroponics method is a less-soil type of farming, and it doesn't require any type of soil. The process involves growing healthy plants without the inclusion of solid medium using nutrients including water solution which is mineral-rich. Hydroponic farming is the subset of hydroculture, and the nutrients used in hydroponic farming systems have different sources.

Monoculture

This method is the raising of a single crop in a specific area of farming. However, in a country like India, the Monoculture technique of farming isn't widely followed. Indoor farming like growing medicinal plants falls under the monoculture. In plain words, monoculture is a modern agriculture practice where a single crop or plant is grown.

Soil levelling advantages

- Ploughing ploughed fields keeps the top fertile soil from being carried away by strong winds or washed away by rainwater.

- The levelling of ploughed soil in the field is accomplished with the use of a Leveller. It is either a heavy wooden or iron plank.

- Ploughed fields that have been levelled aid in the uniform distribution of water in the fields during irrigation.

- The levelling of ploughed fields aids in the prevention of moisture loss.

- Soil manuring

- Manuring is the final step in soil preparation after ploughing and manuring. It aids in the replenishment of rich nutrients to the soil; nitrogen, phosphorus, and potassium are considered the major nutrients, and manuring ensures that they are added to the soil to increase productivity.

Manuring also provides many other nutrients and organic fertilisers. The regular addition of compost and other manure improves soil structure, moisture-holding capacity, soil aeration, and water infiltration.

- **Significance of Soil Manuring**

- Manuring farmland improves soil fertility and crop yield.

- Manure improves soil texture by recycling nitrogen and introducing beneficial bacteria.

- The seeds are nourished by the proper mixing of manure and soil. Manuring is done to replenish the soil with nutrients and thus aid in crop growth.

- **Tools for Soil Preparation**

- Plough: A plough is a simple tool that farmers used in the past. It is triangular in shape and has a sharp pointed edge. Ploughs have traditionally been drawn by animals such as oxen, bulls, and so on. It is made up of three parts: the beam, the ploughshare, and the plough shaft.

Hoe: A hoe is a simple tool for removing weeds and loosening the soil. It has a long wooden handle that is attached to various styles of iron blades. Animals in the agricultural fields also pull it.

Cultivator: A cultivator is a sophisticated agricultural tool. It saves a significant amount of time, labour, and energy. It is used with a tractor.

Levelling (or Leveling) is a branch of surveying, the object of which is: i) to find the elevations of given points with respect to a given or assumed datum, and ii) to establish points at a given or assumed datum. The first operation is required to enable the works to be designed while the second operation is required in the setting out of all kinds of engineering works. Levelling deals with measurements in a vertical plane.

Level surface: A level surface is defined as a curved surface which at each point is perpendicular to the direction of gravity at the point. The surface of a still water is a truly level surface. Any surface parallel to the mean spheroidal surface of the earth is, therefore, a level surface.

Level line: A level line is a line lying in a level surface. It is, therefore, normal to the plumb line at all points.

Methods of levelling

Three principle methods are used for determining differences in elevation, namely, barometric levelling, trigonometric levelling and spirit levelling.

Barometric levelling

Barometric levelling makes use of the phenomenon that difference in elevation between two points is proportional to the difference in atmospheric pressures at these points. A barometer, therefore, may be used and the readings observed at different points would yield a measure of the relative elevation of those points.

At a given point, the atmospheric pressure doesn't remain constant in the course of the day, even in the course of an hour. The method is, therefore, relatively inaccurate and is little used in surveying work except on reconnaissance or exploratory survey.

Trigonometric Levelling (Indirect Levelling)

Trigonometric or Indirect levelling is the process of levelling in which the elevations of points are computed from the vertical angles and horizontal distances measured in the field, just as the length of any side in any triangle can be computed from proper trigonometric relations. In a modified form called stadia levelling, commonly used in mapping, both the difference in elevation and the horizontal distance between the points are directly computed from the measured vertical angles and staff readings.

Spirit Levelling (Direct Levelling)

It is that branch of levelling in which the vertical distances with respect to a horizontal line (perpendicular to the direction of gravity) may be used to determine the relative difference in elevation between two adjacent points. A horizontal plane of sight tangent to level surface at any point is readily established by means of a spirit level or a level vial. In spirit levelling, a spirit level and a sighting device (telescope) are combined and vertical distances are measured by observing on graduated rods placed on the points. The method is also known as direct levelling. It is the most precise method of determining elevations and the one most commonly used by engineers.

Manuring: Mixing soil with manure helps increase soil fertility.

Significance of Preparation of Soil

The act of ploughing of land makes the root penetrate deeper into the soil.

Aeration of roots takes place, and the right amount of water and oxygen is supplied.

During the preparation of soil, the unwanted plants or weeds are removed from the soil in the act of ploughing.

The large or harmful organisms are destroyed.

What is Sowing?

Sowing is a process of planting seeds into the soil. During this agricultural process, proper precautions should be taken, including the appropriate depth, proper distance maintained, and soil should be clean, healthy and free from disease and other pathogens including fungus.

Traditional Method

A funnel-shaped tool is used to sow the seeds traditionally. The funnel is filled with seeds and the seeds pass through two or three pipes with sharp ends. These ends enter into the soil and the seeds are placed there.

Broadcasting

In this process, the seeds are scattered on the seed beds either mechanically or manually. In the broadcasting method of sowing, the seeds are spread uniformly and are then covered with planking. When there are a large number of seeds, the work is done using mechanical broadcasters. The seed rate is very high in this system.

Dibbling

Holes are made in the seedbeds and the seeds are placed in it. The seedbeds are then covered. The holes are made at definite depths. A dibbler is used for dibbling. It is a conical instrument that makes proper holes in the seedbed. This method is usually used to sow vegetables.

Drilling

The seeds are dropped into furrow lines in a continuous flow and are then covered with soil. This is done either mechanically or manually. The proper amount of seeds are sown at proper depths and proper spaces. Drilling can be done in the following ways:

Sowing behind the plough

Bullock-drawn seed drills

Tractor-drawn seeds drills

Seed Dropping behind the Plough

This method is commonly used in villages to sow a variety of food crops such as maize, peas, wheat, barley, and gram. Seeds are dropped in furrows behind the plough by a device known as malobansa. It comprises of a bamboo tube with a funnel-shaped mouth. It needs two men to drop the seeds. One handles the bullocks and the plough and the other drops the seeds. However, this method consumes a lot of time and is labour-intensive.

Transplanting

In this process, the seedlings are first planted in nurseries and then planted in the prepared fields. It is usually done to grow vegetables and flowers. A transplanter is used for the purpose. But, this process is time-consuming.

Hill Dropping

In this method of sowing, the selected seeds are dropped at regular spaces but not in a continuous manner.

Check Row Planting

The seeds are planted along straight parallel furrows. A check row planter is used for the method. The row-to-row and plant-to-plant distance is uniform.

IX

Soil

Good, healthy soils are not only critical for crop production, they are also crucial for good nutrition. Soils high in mineral content produce crops with higher levels of those nutrients. Yet in developing countries like India, which struggles to provide its population with nutritious food, there seems to be no real market among farmers for information on soil health. How can that be?

One line of thought attributes this missing market to poor infrastructure. Another speculates that there is simply low demand for such information. To explore this question in greater detail, I spent the summer of 2019 engaging with farmers and other stakeholders in Munger district in Bihar, India, to understand their views on soil health.

A critical step in the quantification of soil quality (SQ) is the selection of SQ benchmarks. The benchmarks used in this study were SQ ratings made by 32 farmer collaborators representing a range of farming systems, scales of operation and geographic locations in the Mid-Atlantic region of USA. Soils from 45 pairs of sites identified by their farmers as having good and poor SQ were sampled over three seasons and analyzed for 19 soil parameters. Farmer judgments of SQ were based on many factors, most commonly soil organic matter, crop performance, soil water availability and erosion history. Selected individual soil parameters were normalized and integrated into an additive SQ index (SQI). Three additional indices were developed using discriminant analysis. The level of agreement between individual parameters, SQIs and farmer SQ ratings was evaluated using paired t-tests and mean percent difference values. The additive SQI was found to have the highest level of agreement with farmer SQ ratings (P<0.0001), demonstrating that a linear combination of soil parameters can be assembled that is more in agreement with holistic SQ criteria, such as farmer SQ ratings, than individual soil parameters. Extractable C from microwave (MW) sterilized soil (a measure of microbial biomass) was the individual parameter that best agreed with farmer SQ ratings (P<0.0001). Five additional soil C parameters, as well as aggregate stability, also agreed well with farmer SQ ratings (all P values <0.0005). The three parameters with the highest ratio of mean percent difference to coefficient of variation (an indication of parameter reliability) were extractable C from MW sterilized soil, anthrone reactive C and macroaggregate stability (14.2, 7.7 and 3.7, respectively). Mineral fertility parameters (pH, Ca, Ca:Mg ratio, P and K) were not significantly related to farmer SQ ratings (P values >0.05). The strong relationships observed between soil C parameters, soil structural parameters and farmer SQ ratings suggest that efforts to improve SQ in the study region should focus on monitoring and enhancement of soil C and soil structure.

www.ingramcontent.com/pod-product-compliance
Lightning Source LLC
Chambersburg PA
CBHW030238150726
47988CB00021B/3070